# CONTENTS

# INTRODUCING *MACBETH*

*Macbeth* is one of Shakespeare's most popular plays. In fact, it's one of the most famous and most performed plays of all time, by any writer. Although short for a Shakespeare play, it's packed with exciting elements: witches and ghosts, blood-soaked battles, murder, madness and revenge.

## Who was Shakespeare?

William Shakespeare is known today as one of the greatest writers who has ever lived. He mostly wrote plays, and lived and worked in England around 400 years ago. Though his language now sounds old-fashioned, his stories are still as popular as ever.

## What's the story?

Macbeth is a good soldier and a loyal servant to King Duncan - or at least, he thought he was! But witchcraft, a power-hungry wife, and Macbeth's own desire for glory lead him towards a deadly decision, from which there is no way back. Read on to begin the blood-soaked story of *Macbeth...*

4

Get **more** out of libraries

**Please return or renew this item by the last date shown.**

**You can renew online at www.hants.gov.uk/library**

**Or by phoning  0300 555 1387**

Hampshire
County Council

Retold by Anna Claybourne

# Illustrated by Tom Morgan-Jones

First published in 2015 by Wayland
Copyright © Wayland 2015

Editor: Elizabeth Brent
Design: Amy McSimpson
Illustration: Tom Morgan-Jones

All rights reserved
Dewey number: 823.9'2-dc23
ISBN: 978 0 7502 8112 6
eBook ISBN: 978 0 7502 8807 1
Library eBook ISBN: 978 0 7502 9344 0

10 9 8 7 6 5 4 3 2 1

Wayland, an imprint of Hachette Children's Group
Part of Hodder & Stoughton
Carmelite House
50 Victoria Embankment
London EC4Y 0DZ

Printed in China

An Hachette UK company
www.hachette.co.uk
www.hachettechildrens.co.uk

WAYLAND
www.waylandbooks.co.uk

# *Macbeth*: Who's who?

At the start of every Shakespeare play is a list of characters, called the *dramatis personae*.

Macduff

A Scottish nobleman

 husband of

Lady Macduff

**Three witches**

Supernatural figures who play a big part in Macbeth's destiny

Banquo

A Scottish nobleman

 father of ⟹ Fleance

↑ friend of

Macbeth

A Scottish nobleman

 husband of ⟶

Lady Macbeth

Macbeth's scheming wife

↓ cousin of

Duncan

The kindly old king of Scotland

 father of ⟶

Malcolm and Donalbane

Duncan's sons, and heirs to the throne

Servants, Gatekeeper, Doctor, Soldiers, Lady-in-waiting

All Shakespeare plays have lots of smaller characters like these.

5

# Chapter One

Thunder and lightning crashed across the sky, and mists swirled over the murky moors, as a deadly battle raged in the valley below. Scotland's forces were fighting off not one but two fearsome foes – the Irish rebel MacDonwald and his men, and an invading army from Norway.

The Scots were outnumbered. But, led on
by their brave generals Banquo and Macbeth,
they battled with grim resolve.
Slowly but surely, they
forced their enemies back.

High on the heath above, huddled against the fog
and freezing rain, crouched three dark,
cloaked figures. Witches.

"This battle will be lost and won by sunset,"
croaked one.

"Let's meet again at dusk, upon the heath,"
cried the second witch.

"And there, on his way home, we'll catch Macbeth!"
cackled the third.

The witches gathered their black cloaks
around them, and vanished into the storm.

Fair is foul and foul is fair.
Hover through the fog and filthy air!

### What does that mean!?
"Fair" means beautiful and "foul" means horrible or evil. The witches are saying that good and bad will get muddled up and swap places.

In the Scottish camp, King Duncan waited anxiously for news of the battle. He was an old man, far too frail to fight – but his beloved sons, Malcolm and Donalbane, were both on the battlefield.

Just then, Malcolm stumbled in, supporting a badly bleeding soldier. "Father!" he panted. "This man saved my life. He can tell you how the battle goes. It's good news!"

The soldier slumped to his knees, but reached up to grasp the king's hand, eager to tell his story.

"Your Majesty," he whispered, "we are winning! Brave Macbeth fought his way forward until he faced MacDonwald – then slashed him open with his sword, and sliced his head off! Ireland retreated, but Norway attacked again. Yet Macbeth and Banquo fought harder than ever. Blood flowed like water..."

The soldier was growing weak. As he was carried away to have his wounds tended, Lord Ross came striding into the camp.

"The war is over, Your Majesty!" Ross announced. "Macbeth is a true hero – he's just led our men to victory against Norway!"

"Worthy Macbeth!" cried Duncan. "He must be rewarded. Find him at once, and tell him he is no longer just the Thane of Glamis. I'm making him Thane of Cawdor too. All the castles and lands of Cawdor shall be his."

"At once, sir!" said Ross, and hurried away.

On the heath, the witches waited. Soon, two men in bloodstained armour came walking wearily towards them.

Macbeth sighed. "I've never known such a horrific, yet happy day," he said. Banquo nodded. Then he stopped, peering into the mist. "Who's there?" he demanded.

The witches were silent. They placed their thin, wizened fingers upon their thin, wizened lips.

"Speak!" Macbeth shouted into the gloom.

"All hail, Macbeth," replied the first witch at last. "Thane of Glamis."

"All hail, Macbeth," said the second, smirking a little. "Thane of Cawdor."

"All hail, Macbeth," called the third witch, "who shalt be king hereafter."

**What does that mean!?**
The phrase "all hail" means greetings! Macbeth is already the "thane", or lord, of Glamis, a part of Scotland. The witches also greet him as the Thane of Cawdor, and as a future king.

Macbeth stared at them in confusion. "What?" he demanded.
"I am Macbeth, Thane of Glamis. Not Cawdor, nor king."

"Ignore them," Banquo said. "They're clearly witches, and not to
be trusted. So, witches," he challenged them, "you've had plenty
to say to Macbeth. What about me, eh?"

"Banquo!" hissed the first
witch's voice again.
"A father of kings..."

"But not a king yourself,"
added another.

Banquo shrugged
disbelievingly. "Come on,
Macbeth. The king wants to see us."

"Wait!" Macbeth cried, staring into the mist.
"What do you mean, Cawdor? What do you mean, king?
How can you know this!?"

But the witches had disappeared.

"Macbeth! Banquo!" Someone was scrambling up the hill
towards them. It was Lord Ross. "The king awaits you,
good sirs. And Macbeth, I have news. For your bravery
in battle, Duncan has made you Thane of Cawdor!"

Macbeth and Banquo stared at each other in amazement.

As they all tramped down the hill, Macbeth whispered to
Banquo, "It came true! What if they were right about you
too – you could be a father of kings!"

"And you could become king yourself," agreed Banquo.
"But Macbeth, don't put your trust in witches.
They could mean to harm you."

But Macbeth couldn't stop thinking about the witches' words. He was King Duncan's cousin, and third in line to the throne after the king's two sons.

He hardly dared to think it, but one truth was staring him in the face. If they were all to die, the crown would be his...

"Macbeth! My worthy cousin!" King Duncan hugged Macbeth tightly. "My nation and crown are safe, thanks to your bravery," the white-haired king exclaimed.

"I am merely your loyal servant," Macbeth said politely.

"To show my gratitude," Duncan went on, "let me pay you and your wife a royal visit – tonight, at your castle in Inverness. We will arrive at sunset."

"T-tonight!?" Macbeth spluttered. "I mean – Your Majesty,
I am honoured! I must send word to my wife at once!"

He hurried away, with the king smiling proudly after him.

In a tapestry-lined room sat a beautiful, raven-haired
woman in a blood-red velvet gown. Her name was Lady
Macbeth, and in her hands she held a letter, delivered to
her that very moment by Macbeth's messenger. Her green
eyes sparkled as she read it.

*My dearest,*

*Wonderful news – the war is won, and I will
soon be home!*

*But something strange happened after the last battle.
Banquo and I met three witches on the heath, who hailed
me Thane of Glamis, Thane of Cawdor, and a future
king! Just moments later, I heard that I had been made
Thane of Cawdor! The witches had spoken the truth!
What if they are right, and I become king too?
You, my darling, will be Queen of Scotland!*

*Yours in haste,*

*Macbeth*

Just then, Lady Macbeth heard footsteps hurrying up the castle
staircase, and a maidservant burst into the room.

"Your Ladyship," she panted, "King Duncan is coming to stay
here tonight! Macbeth is on his way, and the king arrives
at sunset!"

Lady Macbeth told her servants to prepare a royal feast.
Then she smoothed out the letter, and read it once more.

"Queen of Scotland," she smiled. "All it will take is a little planning. Macbeth may be too weak, too well-meaning, to do what's required. But I'm made of sterner stuff. I'll fill myself with cruelty, and then, under cover of darkness, I'll make sure that crown is ours."

Just then, her husband himself arrived.

"My beloved Thane of Glamis," she cried, leaping up to greet him. "My noble Thane of Cawdor – and perhaps, something even greater, before long!

"My darling..." said Macbeth. "King Duncan is coming here – tonight."

"Ah, yes, I know," his wife replied. "And he won't be leaving, will he? Come on, Macbeth – I can read your face like a book. You're thinking what I'm thinking. Tonight is our chance. Make sure you play the welcoming host, to cover our tracks."

"But... he's our guest!"

Lady Macbeth ignored him. "Just leave it all to me," she said.

Bear welcome in your eye, Your hand, your tongue; look like the innocent flower, But be the serpent under it.

## What does that mean!?

Lady Macbeth tells her husband to "bear welcome", or be welcoming, and appear innocent even though he is planning an evil act, like a deadly snake hiding under a flower.

King Duncan arrived as planned, along
with his sons, his noblemen and servants.
Before long, the royal feast was under way,
and everyone was having a wonderful
time – except Macbeth.

"I can't kill Duncan," he groaned to himself.
"Not in my own castle."

"What's the matter with you!?" hissed his wife.

"We can't do this," said Macbeth. "Forget being king.
I'm happy as we are."

"Don't be stupid!" Lady Macbeth snapped. "Are you a coward?
A real man would do it!"

"I am a real man... just not a murderer. And what if it
doesn't work?"

"Oh, stop fussing. It'll be fine, as long as you do what I say.
Duncan has two bodyguards – I'll make sure they have plenty
of wine and fall fast asleep. At midnight, you go to his chamber,
use their daggers on Duncan, then put them back. It will look
as if they did it. Simple!"

# Chapter Two

The moon was down, and the castle was bathed in darkness
aas Macbeth crept across the courtyard.

"Who goes there!?" Macbeth jumped. It was Banquo, coming
the other way with a lantern.

"Just me... making sure everyone's tucked up safely!"
said Macbeth.

"Ah, Macbeth! You should be in bed too! You've done the king
proud – that was a wonderful feast. Goodnight – see you in the
morning."

Then Banquo was gone,
and the darkness
descended again.
Nothing now kept
Macbeth from his
terrible task.

He turned towards the tower where Duncan slept – then stopped. Something was glinting in the gloom, in front of his eyes. He peered harder and saw a dagger, hovering in mid-air.

"What are you?" Macbeth whispered. He tried to touch the dagger, but his hand felt nothing. As he stared, drops of blood began to drip from the blade.

"It's not real," Macbeth trembled. "My mind's playing tricks on me." He put his head down and walked on.

Is this a **dagger** which
I see before me,
The handle toward my hand?
Come, let me **clutch** thee!

In her room, Lady Macbeth paced up and down, waiting.

"What was that!?" She jumped at a noise. But it was just an owl, hooting on the battlements.

Then Macbeth came in. By candlelight, she could see that his hands were covered in blood, and he was carrying the bodyguards' daggers. His face was hollow and haunted.

"I've done it," he said.

"Why have you brought the daggers here?" she demanded. "You should have put them back in the guards' hands!"

"I can't go back again," said Macbeth. "I daren't look at what I did."

"I'll do it," said Lady Macbeth impatiently, snatching the daggers. "Go and wash that blood off."

But although he washed, and put on a fresh, white nightgown, Macbeth felt that his hands would never be clean again.

Not long after the sun came up, there was a loud knocking at the castle doors. It was Macduff, the Thane of Fife, and his friend Lord Lennox. They had an appointment with the king that day.

"Knock, knock, knock!" grumbled the gatekeeper, who had drunk far too much the night before, and had a terrible headache. "Hang on a minute, will you!"

He stumbled to his feet, fumbling for the castle keys. "Knock, knock – I heard you the first time! I'm coming!" He opened the huge castle doors, blinking as the sunlight struck him in the face. "Who is it?"

"It's me, Macduff. I'm here to see the king. Where is his room? I'll go and wake him myself."

The gatekeeper pointed the visitors to the royal chamber, and settled down for another snooze. But only a minute later, a terrible cry rang out from the direction of the tower.

"Noooo!!" screamed Macduff's voice. "Murder and treason! Malcolm, Donalbane, Banquo!"

Murder and treason! Banquo and Donalbane! Malcolm! Awake! Shake off this downy sleep, death's counterfeit, And look on death itself!

## What does that mean!?

As Macduff wakes the others with the horrible news, he describes sleep as a "counterfeit" or pretend death, falsely comforting everyone, when there is a real death in their midst.

Macduff's shouting soon woke up the whole castle. Lady Macbeth emerged from her room in her nightdress, looking puzzled. Banquo, Malcolm and Donalbane appeared too.

"The king is dead!" wailed Macduff. "Murdered in his sleep!"

28

Macbeth came in, looking shocked. "It's true," he said.
"I've just been to the king's room. It seems it was his
bodyguards – they were covered in blood. I was so furious,
I killed them, there and then!"

"Oh! help!" Lady Macbeth distracted everyone's attention
by falling down in a faint.

"Look to the lady!" said Macduff, and everyone rushed
to help her.

Amidst the kerfuffle, Prince Malcolm took his younger
brother aside.

"I'm scared, Donalbane," he said. "I don't believe his
bodyguards did it. Someone plotted against our father,
and we'll be next. Let's get out of here."

No one noticed as the two brothers made a quick exit,
and rode away into the sunlit countryside.

With Duncan dead, and his two sons nowhere to be found,
Scotland lacked a king. Indeed, gossip began to spread that,
as they had run away, Malcolm and Donalbane must be
responsible for the murder. Some said they had bribed
the bodyguards to do the deed.

As the king's cousin, Macbeth was the next in line. Before
long, he found himself sitting on the throne, having a gold and
ermine crown placed upon
his head. Beside him,
his wife, the Queen
of Scotland, smiled
graciously, as she too
received her crown
and royal robes.

But there was one
person Macbeth
needed to speak
to – his old friend
Banquo. Banquo knew
what the witches had
said, and Macbeth
wanted to see if he
suspected anything.
He summoned him
for a meeting.

# Chapter Three

Banquo couldn't help feeling a little uncomfortable
as he waited in a huge palace room to see the new king.

"Well, Macbeth," he mumbled to himself. "
It did all come true. You're Thane
of Glamis, Thane of Cawdor,
and king as well. But I'm
a bit worried about how
it all fell into place.
Something doesn't
seem quite right..."

At that moment, the gilded
doors swung open, and in
swept Macbeth, his wife,
lords and servants.

"Ah, Banquo, how nice to
see you," said Macbeth.
Banquo spun around
nervously.

"My wife and I are holding a grand dinner
party this evening. We'd love you to come."

"Well... of course I will," said Banquo, with fake politeness.
He had expected a chat with his friend, not the whole royal
entourage!

"I'm going riding this afternoon, with my son Fleance,"
Banquo managed to add. "But I'll be back in time for dinner."

"Excellent," said Macbeth. But behind his royal smile,
he began to panic.

"Banquo knows something," he scowled to himself. "I can't let
my secret get out. And what's more, if the witches were right,
Banquo's sons will one day take my place. I have to stop him."

Making sure the coast was clear, he sent for three assassins.
He had a little job for them.

That evening, lights burned in the palace
as the cooks prepared food for Macbeth's
party, and the guests began to gather.
The sun had set by the time Banquo
and Fleance returned from their ride.

As they tied up their horses, there was
a rustling sound behind them, and
three men leapt out of the bushes.

Suddenly Banquo felt himself being grabbed from behind, and a knife blade was plunged into the back of his neck.

"Aarrgh... murder!" he gulped, sinking to his knees.

"Father!" cried Fleance. He turned to face the shadowy men.

"No, Fleance, they'll get you too – run away!" gasped Banquo, with his dying breath. Fleance stumbled off and escaped into the night.

It was time for dinner. The guests were seated around the table, but two chairs were still empty – Macbeth's and Banquo's. For some reason, Macbeth had been called away. Lady Macbeth made polite conversation.

"It's done, sir," the assassin whispered to Macbeth, outside the door. "Banquo's dead.""And Fleance?"

"Er, no sir, sorry. Fleance got away."

Macbeth wanted to curse the man, but he had to get back to his guests. He sent the assassin away.

When he turned back to the table, however, he stopped short in horror. There was Banquo, right in front of him. Sitting in his seat at the table. Covered in blood, with stab wounds all over his neck and head.

"What!?" the king gasped. "W-what are you doing there!?"

Banquo smiled calmly at Macbeth, blood dripping from his hair.

"It wasn't me!!!" screamed Macbeth. "You can't say it was me! Get out of my sight! You're not real! Get away!"

Everyone was staring at Macbeth in alarm. "Do excuse my husband," said Lady Macbeth hurriedly. "He's just a little tired."

Thou canst **not** say I did it. Never shake Thy **gory** locks at me!

**What does that mean!?**
When Macbeth sees Banquo's
ghost, he claims he was not
the killer (because he used
hired assassins). "Don't
shake your blood-soaked hair
at me!" he cries.

"The king doesn't seem very well," said Lord Ross nervously. Macbeth's words were very worrying indeed.
"I think we should leave."

"No, no!" Lady Macbeth said, "Don't trouble yourselves... sit down."

"It's Banquo!!! CAN'T YOU SEE HIM?!" screamed Macbeth. "He's right there! There!! Look!!"

Banquo got up and glided away, but only Macbeth watched him go. No one else could see him.

"Perhaps we should postpone the dinner party after all," said Lady Macbeth. "I'm so sorry."

The guests couldn't get up fast enough. They stumbled over each other on their way to the door.

"I wish the king better health," called Lord Lennox
over his shoulder.

"What's wrong with you?" Lady Macbeth demanded,
as the door closed behind them. "Are you insane!?"

"Blood will have blood," said Macbeth, shaking in terror.
"Murder leads to more murder, and where does it ever end?
I've hardly even got started. What about Macduff? What about
him!? He didn't come to the dinner. I bet he suspects something
too! I'll go and see the witches again. I need to know what
happens next. I'm so deeply soaked in blood now, I might
as well keep going, and kill whoever stands in my path."
Lady Macbeth took his hand.

# "Calm down,"

she said. "Stop this. You need to sleep." And she led him away.

The next day, Lord Lennox was talking to a friend in private.

"Well, Macbeth's reign is turning out to be more than a little strange," he sighed. "First Duncan died – then poor Banquo. It's hardly safe to be out at night! I hope Macduff doesn't decide to go out riding too. Since he didn't go to the feast, he's in the king's bad books! Do you know where Macduff is now?"

"I do," said his friend. "He's in England, visiting Malcolm. Because I think you and I both know Malcolm had nothing to do with Duncan's death, and nor did Donalbane. Right now, Macduff and Malcolm are getting an army together. They plan to attack Scotland, and restore this country to its rightful king."

"I just hope Macduff can escape Macbeth's clutches,"
said Lennox, "and help Malcolm claim the throne!"

# Chapter Four

At that moment, Macbeth himself was nowhere near the palace.
He was high on the heath, huddling his cloak around him,
tramping towards the place where he had first seen the witches.

The three witches were waiting for him. They were conjuring up a powerful spell, to predict Macbeth's future once more. Around a boiling cauldron, they danced and whirled, throwing in frogs' toes and newts' eyes, wolves' teeth and rotten tufts of bats' wool. The cauldron smoked and spat, and the witches sang:

Double, double, toil and trouble,
fire burn and cauldron bubble...

"By the pricking of my thumbs," one witch cried. "Something wicked this way comes!"

She meant Macbeth, who now strode up to them. "Witches!" he called. "I need to ask you something."

"We know what you want. Be silent!" hissed another witch. "Watch the cauldron, and your questions shall be answered."

As Macbeth stared, the shape of a soldier's head, wearing a helmet, arose out of the steaming cauldron. It began to speak, in a hoarse, bloodcurdling voice:

"Macbeth, Macbeth, Macbeth! Beware Macduff!"

41

I knew it!" said Macbeth. "Macduff! I knew it!"
"Hush!" whispered a witch in his ear. "Watch!"

The soldier had gone, and now Macbeth saw the shape
of a baby, covered in blood.

"None of woman born shall harm Macbeth," the baby said,
in a small voice.

Macbeth began to breathe again. "Then I'm safe," he said. "For everyone who walks the Earth was born from their mother."

At last, a third vision appeared. It was a child, wearing a crown and carrying a branch. It spoke:

"Macbeth shall never vanquished be until Great Birnam Wood walks to Dunsinane Hill."
Macbeth felt giddy with relief. "A wood can't walk," he laughed. "What nonsense!"

But when he turned to the witches, they were gone. Coming towards him was Lord Lennox.

"Sir, I bring news," Lennox said nervously. No one wanted to upset the king, but Macbeth had been demanding to know where Macduff was. "It seems Macduff is in England, sir."

"Gone to England!?" growled Macbeth. "Has he, now? Right. I'll show that traitor a thing or two."

Lady Macduff missed her husband, but she was also angry. He might have important business in London, but he had left her and her children alone, at the mercy of Macbeth.

"Macduff is only doing what he thinks best," said Lord Ross kindly, when he came to visit her in her castle. "These are dangerous times, and someone must do something. Your husband is a brave man."

After Lord Ross had left, Lady Macduff turned to her young son. "How will we survive now?" she asked tearfully.

"Like the birds do, mother," he said.

"What, eating worms!?"
Lady Macduff laughed.

"We'll just survive any way we can, that's what I mean," the boy smiled, giving her a hug.

"My lady!" A strange man stood in the doorway. Lady Macduff
held her son tighter.

"I mean no harm, Your Ladyship. I know you don't know me,
and I'm just a poor workman – but I must warn you, madam.
I have seen soldiers riding this way. You must hide!"

Lady Macduff took her son's hand, and got up to run and find
her other children. But she was too late. She heard voices in the
passageway, and a second later Macbeth's men, their daggers
raised, ran into the room.

In England, Macduff and Malcolm had gathered ten thousand men, ready to march on Scotland.

"My only fear is," Malcolm confessed, "I'm not fit to rule Scotland. I'm not the man my father was."

"Scotland cries out for its true leader, Malcolm," said Macduff. "And even if you don't match Duncan, you'll be a hundred times better than Macbeth..."

Just then, a servant ushered in a visitor.

"Ross!" cried Macduff. "You've joined us! What news from Scotland!?"

Lord Ross swallowed. He looked pale.

"I'm afraid I have bad news, Macduff," he said quietly. "The very worst. I'm so sorry..." Macduff stared at him.

What, all my pretty chickens and their dam, in one fell swoop?

"Macbeth sent his men to your castle..." Lord Ross mumbled. "Your wife and children... they're dead. Murdered."

"My children...?" Macduff whispered. Lord Ross nodded.

"My wife?" Malcolm put a hand on Macduff's shoulder. Macduff sank to his knees. "All of them...?"

"Macduff," said Malcolm. "Macbeth must be stopped. Let this cruel crime spur us on. We must go now, and free Scotland from this reign of terror – and you can take your revenge."

"I will avenge them," Macduff said, white with pain and fury. "I will hunt Macbeth down, until we are face to face, and he stands within my sword's reach. What are we waiting for?"

# Chapter Five

Scotland had many castles, but the mightiest of them all was Dunsinane. Macbeth had barricaded himself, his wife and his last few loyal servants and soldiers inside its towering walls.

However, Lady Macbeth was far from well. Every night, past midnight, she roamed the candlelit halls, sleepwalking and murmuring strange words to herself. The doctor could do little to help.

"She's coming, sir," whispered a lady-in-waiting, as the doctor sat up late to see what was happening.

Lady Macbeth walked towards them slowly, in her long, white nightgown, her eyes staring vacantly.

"She's awake," said the doctor.

"No, sir – her eyes are open, but she doesn't see us."

Lady Macbeth rubbed her hands over and over each other. "Will these hands never be clean?" she asked. "Look, here's a spot of blood. And another. Get off me, bloodstains, off! These hands smell of blood. No perfume can sweeten them!"

"She has a troubled mind," said the doctor, "and has seen things she should not!"

"Aye," said the lady-in-waiting. "I wouldn't take her place – not for anything."

Out, damned spot! Out I say!

### What does that mean!?
In this famous line, Lady Macbeth orders the blood spot she thinks she can see to leave her hand.

As Malcolm and Macduff led their army
north from England, Scotland's thanes
and lords gathered with their own
men. None of them could support
Macbeth any longer. They planned
to join forces with the English army,
and rise up against the tyrant's rule.

"Let us all swear allegiance,"
cried Lord Lennox, "not to our king,
Macbeth, but to Malcolm, our king-to-
be. Birnam Wood is the meeting place.
From there, under Malcolm's command,
we will attack Dunsinane!"

50

In Dunsinane Castle, Macbeth's servants scurried around him nervously.

"Let the English come!" the king roared. "I'm not scared! They were all born from their mothers, weren't they!? So they can't hurt me! And I can't be harmed until Birnam Wood WALKS to Dunsinane, can I? What!?" he yelled at a white-faced message boy. "What is it?!"

"Your Majesty, the English are almost here, sir. We have word there are ten thousand men, sir."

"SCARED, ARE YOU!?" Macbeth screamed at him, and the boy backed out of the room.

At that moment, the doctor came in. "Your Majesty," he began. "I'm afraid to say your wife is very ill indeed..."

"So cure her!" Macbeth shouted. "Go and do your job!"

Then Macbeth sent everyone away, calling for only his most-trusted manservant, Seyton. As he waited alone, he suddenly sank down onto a bench and stared helplessly at his hands.

"Maybe I cannot be killed," he said quietly to himself, "but what's the point in living any more? At my age, a man should have faithful old friends, loyal servants, a loving family.

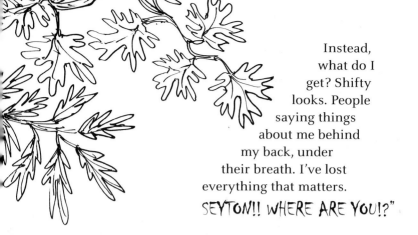

Instead, what do I get? Shifty looks. People saying things about me behind my back, under their breath. I've lost everything that matters.

SEYTON!! WHERE ARE YOU!?"

As Seyton hurried in and fussed over Macbeth's armour, sunshine filtered through the leafy branches of nearby Birnam Wood. There, thousands upon thousands of soldiers stood at the ready – their helmets on, their swords sharp and bright, their ears eager for Malcolm's command.

"Macbeth thinks there are ten thousand of us," Malcolm's voice rang out. "But with the Scots, we number many more.

"Let's keep our enemy in the dark until the last minute. To hide the truth, let each man cut a bough from this great forest. We'll march with the branches above our heads, so no one will be able to count us. Then, as we approach Dunsinane Castle, wait for my orders."

What does that mean!?
"Hew" means cut and
"bear" means carry.

"Prepare to fight!!" Macbeth yelled at his servants and soldiers. "Come on, you cowards! This is Dunsinane Castle – it can withstand any attack!"

Then they all heard a wailing sound from the royal bedroom. Seyton came in. "Macbeth," he said, as calmly as he could. "I'm sorry. The queen is dead."

Everyone waited for the king to scream and curse, but he was silent. Then he whispered, "She died too soon. This isn't the time for such news." He stared at the ground.

"Life is nothing, really, is it?" Macbeth went on, sadly, as everyone held their breath. "It's no more than being an actor on a stage, wandering around for an hour, then going off again. It's nothing more than the meaningless rantings of an idiot."

### What does that mean!?
Macbeth compares human life to acting on a stage - which, of course, would be actually happening during a performance of the play. A "player" is Shakespeare's word for an actor.

Suddenly, in burst a breathless messenger who had been keeping watch outside.

"Your Majesty," he gasped, "you'll never believe it!"

"What? What is it, man!?"

"I was keeping watch, looking towards Birnam Wood, and... well, sir, the wood is moving! It's coming towards us!"

"LIAR!!" Macbeth roared.

"I swear... go and see for yourself, Your Majesty!"

"Enough of this nonsense," Macbeth growled. "We have a battle to fight. Swords at the ready – we're going out!" And he drew his gleaming sword from its sheath, and strode out to the castle gates.

"Halt!" cried Malcolm, as his men, carrying their rustling boughs, came to the top of Dunsinane Hill. "This is the place. On my word, throw down your branches, and storm the castle. GO!!!"

Just as he had bravely fought the Irish and the Norwegians, Macbeth battled his attackers with courage and cunning. Every soldier in his path tried to fight him, but they were no match for his skill and strength.

To left and right, they lay dead, slashed and slaughtered
by his bloody sword.

But Macbeth could not take on every man in the army.
Malcolm's forces surrounded him and his soldiers, swarming
into Dunsinane Castle. They won the battle easily. All that
remained was to kill the king himself. And only one man
could do that.

"Turn!" came a voice from behind Macbeth. "Turn and fight me, hound of hell!"

Macbeth spun around. "Macduff," he gasped.

"Words can't express how evil you are," Macduff snarled, "so I'll let my sword speak for me. Die, murdering scum!"

"Don't bother," taunted Macbeth, as he blocked Macduff's blows. "Birnam Wood may have come to Dunsinane – but you still can't kill me. The witches told me no man of woman born can harm Macbeth."

"Coward!" Macduff yelled. "I'm afraid your witches left out one little fact, Macbeth. Macduff was never born. My mother died before my birth, and I was cut from her dead body, to save my life."

"NO!!" screamed Macbeth. "I will never give in!"

So Macduff, more furious and fevered than ever, fought on, until he forced Macbeth to the ground, stood on his chest, and sliced his head off.

Malcolm looked up to see Macduff, holding Macbeth's severed head by its matted, blood-drenched hair. "Macbeth is dead. His evil reign is over. Welcome home, King Malcolm!"

# "Hail, King of Scotland!"

# MACBETH AT A GLANCE

*Macbeth* has just over 2,100 lines of text, making it one of Shakespeare's shortest plays. The action is fast and furious, jumping quickly from one scene to the next.

**FACT FILE:**
FULL TITLE: The Tragedy of Macbeth
DATE WRITTEN: around 1606
LENGTH: 2,113 lines

## Macbeth as a play

The retelling in this book is written in prose, like a novel. But Shakespeare wrote *Macbeth* as a play, to be performed on stage. Apart from a few stage directions (instructions for the actors), the play has no descriptions or explanations from the author. It's just dialogue – the words spoken by the characters.

Here you can see what the opening of *Macbeth* looks like, as Shakespeare wrote it:

## ACT 1

Scene 1. [An open place]

Thunder and lightning. Enter three witches. ← Stage directions

FIRST WITCH: When shall we three meet again,
In thunder, lightning, or in rain?

SECOND WITCH: When the hurlyburly's done,
When the battle's lost and won.

# Acts and scenes

Shakespeare divided all his plays into five main sections called acts. These are split into smaller sections called scenes, each set in a different place or room.

Acts and scenes make it easier for actors to learn the play in short chunks. Shakespeare also uses them to give structure to the play's events, as you can see here:

## THE FIVE ACTS OF *MACBETH*

ACT 1 (7 scenes)
Act 1 leads up to the point where
Macbeth resolves to kill King Duncan.

ACT 2 (4 scenes)
The murder of the king and
its discovery take up Act 2.

ACT 3 (6 scenes)
Act 3 is often a turning point in Shakespeare's
tragedies. After Macbeth murders his friend
Banquo, he realises he has become a monster –
while others start to plot against him.

ACT 4 (3 scenes)
During this act, Macbeth's evil
and cruelty reach new heights,
and his downfall is assured.

## ACT 5 **(8 scenes)**

Act 5 rounds up the play – in this case,
with the battle that ends Macbeth's rule,
and his face-to-face fight to the death
with his nemesis, Macduff.

# THE STORY OF *MACBETH*

Shakespeare is famous for his great stories, but he didn't actually make them up himself! He mostly borrowed his plots from history, mythology, or stories from old books. He sometimes changed the details, or combined two stories into one.

## The real Macbeth

Shakespeare based the story of *Macbeth* on a real Scottish king, Mac Bethad (or Macbeth in English). Mac Bethad did kill the previous king, Duncan, then ruled the Scots from 1040–1057. He eventually died in a battle that returned Duncan's son Malcolm to the throne.

## History books

Between the 1000s and Shakespeare's own time, several historians wrote about the real Macbeth. But in those days, history books weren't as accurate as they are now. The main book Shakespeare used, by Raphael Holinshed, included the witches and their predictions, Lady Macbeth's role in the murder, and the moving of Birnam Wood.

The audience loves us!

## Shakespeare's version

Shakespeare changed things even further by making Macbeth's reign shorter and more evil. In the history books, Banquo helped Macbeth murder Duncan, but Shakespeare made him a good character instead. He made the witches more important too – probably as they made such a great spectacle to see on stage!

# Map of *Macbeth*

Shakespeare used real Scottish castles, palaces and battlefields as settings in *Macbeth*, so the action moves around all over Scotland.

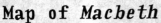

Inverness, where Duncan visits Macbeth in his castle

Forres, location of the opening battle scene

Birnam Wood

Cawdor

Glamis

Dunsinane

Scone, where Macbeth is crowned in the royal palace

Fife, home of Macduff

# SHAKESPEARE AND *MACBETH*

Why did Shakespeare write *Macbeth*?
There were two main reasons: as an
entertainment, and as a message to the king.

## Shakespeare and showbusiness

Shakespeare came from Stratford-upon-Avon in central England,
but lived in London for at least 20 years, from around 1590–1610.
During the reign of Elizabeth I, he became part-owner of
a theatre company, the Chamberlain's Men. He wrote plays for
the company, acted in them, and helped to build theatres too.

Shakespeare's company needed new plays all
the time. He had to find stories that would be
fun to watch and pull in paying audiences.
Comedies needed laughs, mix-ups and funny
characters. Tragedies needed action, emotion,
thrills and horror. The tale of Macbeth – or the
story Shakespeare spun it into – was perfect.

## A trip to the theatre

One theatregoer, Dr Simon Forman, went to see *Macbeth* in 1610, and described it in his diary. He clearly remembered the exciting bits best!

*The blood on his hands could not be washed off...*

"And he, turning about to sit down again, saw the ghost of Banquo..."

"Macbeth slew * Macduff's wife and children".

*killed

## Keeping the King happy

In 1603, after Elizabeth 1 died, King James VI of Scotland also became king of England. He supported Shakespeare's company, who changed their name to the King's Men. Shakespeare used *Macbeth* to show support for James in return.

Banquo was thought to be one of James's ancestors, so the play cast him in a good light. It also warned against trying to get rid of a good ruler. Lastly, it showed the English and Scots working together for a good outcome – something they had to do while sharing a king.

# STAGING *MACBETH*

Shakespeare wrote *Macbeth* to be performed by
his own theatre company, in their own theatre,
the Globe. He might even have acted in it himself.

## Going to the Globe

The Globe was one of several open-air theatres in London
in Shakespeare's time. There were no electric lights, so
plays were shown in the afternoon, while it was still
daylight. Audiences weren't polite or quiet, like today.
They chatted, shouted out rude comments, wandered
around and ate snacks throughout the show.

## Stars of the stage

Shakespeare's theatre company included some of the most
famous actors of the day. Richard Burbage was the star
performer, and was the first actor to play Macbeth. Another
actor, Robert Armin, was known for his comedy roles, and
always played the clown or fool. In *Macbeth*, he would
probably have been the grumpy, drunken gatekeeper.

We don't know if Shakespeare himself acted
in *Macbeth*, but he was said to play "kingly"
roles – so he might have taken a turn as Duncan.

The Globe was built in a tall doughnut shape, with three storeys of seats under the roof around the edge.

There wasn't much scenery. Instead, the characters described their surroundings to set the scene.

In the middle was the stage and an open-air standing area.

MALCOLM:
The wood of Birnam.

LORD:
What wood is this before us?

# *MACBETH:* THEMES AND SYMBOLS

Shakespeare often used repeated themes, images and symbols throughout a play. This helped to highlight particular characters, or reinforce aspects of the story. Here are a few of the main themes and symbols in *Macbeth*:

## Blood

Blood is a symbol of Macbeth and Lady Macbeth's evil deeds and guilty consciences. Both of them feel they have blood on their hands that can never be washed off.

LADY MACBETH:
Out, damned spot!

Later, he says his reign of terror is like wading across a river of blood.

MACBETH:
I am in blood
Stepp'd in so
far that should
I wade no more,
Returning were as
tedious as go o'er.

Macbeth sees a vision of a dagger with blood on the blade.

## Hallucinations and madness

As their guilt gradually drives them insane, Macbeth and Lady Macbeth see things that are not really there. These hallucinations reveal what is preying on their minds.

Macbeth sees a phantom dagger... and the ghost of murdered Banquo.

Lady Macbeth sees spots of blood on her hands, when no one else can.

## Opposites

Two opposite forces, good and bad, struggle inside Macbeth. Opposites often appear in the play to reflect this.

**MACBETH:** So foul and fair a day I have not seen.

**WITCHES:** Fair is foul and foul is fair.

**MACBETH:** This supernatural soliciting Cannot be ill, cannot be good...

## Sleep

Sleep appears in the play as an imitation of death.

Sleeplessness is a symbol of guilt and torment. After murdering Duncan, Macbeth fears he will never sleep again.

**MACDUFF:** Shake off this downy sleep, death's counterfeit.

**MACBETH:** Methought I heard a voice cry, "Sleep no more! Macbeth doth murder sleep."

He tells Lady Macbeth he suffers "terrible dreams", while her own sleep is disturbed by sleepwalking.

71

# WITCHCRAFT

Macbeth's fate is driven by the words of the three witches he meets. In Shakespeare's time, this would have been even scarier than it is now, as many people really believed in witchcraft.

## Witches' work

In the 1500s, people thought witches were servants of the devil. They were said to cast spells and cause illnesses, and could fly, turn invisible, and see the future. Bad harvests and outbreaks of disease were often blamed on witches. They were even said to make milk go off!

## Who were the witches?

Anyone, male or female, could be accused of being a witch, but most so-called witches were women. Older women who lived alone were often targeted, especially if they had pets (thought to be evil assistants or "familiars"). Some were good at making medicines from herbs, and this was seen as similar to mixing potions and casting spells.

Pictures of witches from Shakespeare's time, like this one from a history book, show them as normal women. They didn't have black hats, cloaks and broomsticks – which meant anyone could be accused of being a witch!

# Witch-hunts

When James I came to the throne in England in 1603, he launched a crackdown on witches. From 1604, anyone found guilty of witchcraft could be put to death. Through the early 1600s, fear of witches increased, and hundreds of people were put to death for suspected witchcraft.

## Did you know?

Witch-hunters used some very unfair tests to see if someone was a witch. For example, a suspected witch might be dunked in a pond or river. If she sank, she was innocent. If she floated, she was a witch!

# THE LANGUAGE OF *MACBETH*

Shakespeare wrote his plays mostly in a kind of non-rhyming poetry, called blank verse. In it, he used several kinds of poetic language to make the characters' speeches more powerful, emotional or atmospheric.

You can see some of these in this piece of blank verse from *Macbeth*. It comes from near the end of the play, when Macbeth hears that Lady Macbeth has died.

Repetition: saying a word several times creates an echoing rhythm to reinforce an idea. →

\*Alliteration: pairs or patterns of words with the same first letter.

She should have died hereafter.
There would have been a time for such a word.
Tomorrow, and tomorrow, and tomorrow,
Creeps in this petty pace* from day to day
To the last syllable of recorded time,
And all our yesterdays have lighted fools
The way to dusty death*. Out, out, brief candle!
Life's but a walking shadow, a poor player
That struts and frets** his hour upon the stage
And then is heard no more. It is a tale
Told by an idiot, full of sound and fury,
Signifying nothing.

\*\*Assonance: groups of words with similar sounds, like "struts" and "frets".

Metaphors: something is described by comparing it to something else – here, Macbeth says life is an actor on the stage and a story that makes no sense.

## Natural speech

Shakespeare sometimes uses more natural, everyday
language too, written in prose, not verse. For example,
it can be used for comedy scenes, moments of shock,
or for the speech of servants, like Lady Macbeth's
lady-in-waiting:

I have seen her rise from her bed,
throw her nightgown upon her, unlock
her closet, take forth paper, fold it,
write upon it, read it, afterwards seal
it, and return again to bed; yet all
this while in a most fast sleep!

## Did you know?

Shakespeare also made up quite a few
new words in his plays. Words and
phrases that first appear in Macbeth
include "fitful", "assassination",
"unreal", and "a sorry sight".

# *MACBETH'S* MEANING NOW

*Macbeth* is more than 400 years old. It was written in a very different society to the one we have now. Yet people still love seeing it. It's been made into films, TV shows and graphic novels – and whatever form it's in, we still find it exciting.

## For all time

After Shakespeare died, his friend Ben Jonson wrote that "He was not of an age, but for all time."

In other words, Shakespeare was brilliant at writing about things that affect everyone, and that will always be important to us. In *Macbeth*, these things include:

## Power

In every age, there are leaders and those who want to lead, and power struggles between them. Macbeth uses evil to win power, then becomes a tyrant – and the same still happens in some countries today. All over the world, people are waging wars to win control, as they do in *Macbeth*.

# Friendship

When Macbeth murders Banquo, he sacrifices his best friend to try and keep his crown. By the time he realises that friendship and love matter more than wealth and power, it's far too late. Whether you're a leader who needs good advice, or just making friends in the playground, this is a lesson people still learn every day.

# Fear of the supernatural

Humans just can't help being interested in ghosts, witches, magic and other supernatural forces – even if we don't really believe in them. From *Harry Potter* to the *Twilight* series, today's bestselling books and films show these themes are just as popular as ever. The supernatural appeals to our deep human fear and fascination for the unknown, and always draws crowds. Shakespeare knew that!

# GLOSSARY

| | |
|---|---|
| **alliteration** | Grouping together words with the same initial letter |
| **ancestor** | A relative who lived long ago |
| **assassin** | A hired killer |
| **assonance** | Grouping together words that sound similar |
| **blank verse** | A type of non-rhyming poetry used by Shakespeare |
| **chamber** | A room |
| **conscience** | A sense of right and wrong about your own behaviour |
| *dramatis personae* | A list of characters in a play |
| **ermine** | White fur from a stoat |
| **familiar** | A witch's animal helper |
| **hallucination** | A vision of something that does not really exist |
| **metaphor** | Describing something as another thing to compare them |
| **nemesis** | The person or thing that will cause your downfall |
| **prose** | Text written in ordinary sentences, not in verse |
| **spectacle** | Something amazing or exciting to look at |
| **stage directions** | Instructions for the actors in a play |
| **supernatural** | Magical or beyond the laws of nature |
| **superstition** | Fear or belief about luck, magic or the supernatural |
| **symbol** | Something that stands for an idea or object |
| **tyrant** | A harsh ruler who destroys those who disagree with them |

# GLOSSARY OF SHAKESPEARE'S LANGUAGE

| | |
|---|---|
| counterfeit | imitation or fake |
| dam | mother |
| doth | does |
| fell | deadly |
| foul | evil or horrible |
| gory | bloody |
| hail | greetings |
| hurlyburly | commotion or struggle |
| o'er | over |
| locks | hair |
| soliciting | persuading or offering |
| thane | a kind of lord |

# MACBETH QUIZ

Test yourself and your friends on the story, characters and language of Shakespeare's *Macbeth*. You can find the answers at the bottom of the page.

1) What is the name of the Irish rebel leader killed by Macbeth at the start of the play?

2) At the start of the play, Macbeth is third in line to the throne. Who are first and second?

3) What title does Duncan award to Macbeth, just as the witches predict?

4) What gives Lady Macbeth a fright in the night as she waits for Macbeth to murder Duncan?

5) Who comes knocking at the castle door the morning after the murder?

6) What is Banquo's son called?

7) Which two people does Lady Macduff talk to just before she is murdered?

8) What vision rises out of the cauldron to warn Macbeth about Birnam Wood coming to Dunsinane?

9) What does Lady Macbeth say to a bloodstain she sees on her hand?

10) What is the name of Macbeth's favourite servant?

**MACBETH**

978 0 7502 8112 6

**HAMLET**

978 0 7502 8117 1

**A MIDSUMMER NIGHT'S DREAM**

978 0 7502 8113 3

**THE TEMPEST**

978 0 7502 8115 7

**ROMEO AND JULIET**

978 0 7502 8114 0

**MUCH ADO ABOUT NOTHING**

978 0 7502 8116 4